February's Country

Poems

Noel-Anne Brennan

Some poems have previously appeared in The Northeast Journal, SageWoman, Circle, Nine Apples, and Essence.

Copyright 2011
All rights reserved.
Sander Press

February's Country

February's Country

Blue light on snow.

Cold, bitter cold,

A brittle twilight burning

With saffron and rose

And the thin black ice

Of the gathering night.

February's country:

Perfection of stillness.

Out of the woods

The full moon rises,

Gliding up through barren branches,

Noel-Anne Brennan

Gold.

The tracks of the hunters

Tic-tac the snow,

Fox and cat and crow.

And now mine

Among them,

In February's country.

February's Country

Early Thaw

In the sudden pale warmth

The world has turned to water.

The snows liquefy

And the dawns

Are white with fog.

Puddles are everywhere:

Water and and ice, reflecting

Pale sun, bare trees.

It feels like spring

But isn't. Winds whisper

Cold, in the early dusk.

Noel-Anne Brennan

But for these days

There is a vision:

Pale sky, watered land,

Of other horizons,

Other dreams

Beyond the chink

Of winter's bitter door.

February's Country

Spring

Spring runs through me
Like a green river;
The ice will melt,
The ice is melting;
I feel the gold sun.
Laughter runs silver,
The season turns
Beneath the young moon;
Spring is a green river
In my mind.

Noel-Anne Brennan

New seeds of life

Grow up

And up.

I feel the gold sun.

February's Country

April

April, country of stars.
Your evenings spin
Soft lavender across the skies,
A-bloom with the silver moon
And all the stars gleaming
Like daffodils among the rocks.
April, land of dreams.
Dreams drift like mists
On the greening meadows,
Swell like buds
On the lilac trees,

Noel-Anne Brennan

Not yet ready

To open to the sun.

April, country of stars

And land of dreams,

I wander here

As if your mists and suns

Could last forever,

Could keep me between

Winter's barrens

And summer's burning,

Safe with promise

Always.

February's Country

Summer

Summer:
Breathless and sultry,
A dream of hazy mornings
And blazing noons,
Of flowers that gleam
Like stars,
Pale moons
In the thickened dusk.
But even as summer hums

Noel-Anne Brennan

Her rich contralto,

The first leaves fall,

Yellow

Into that breathless song.

February's Country

November: The Message

We have entered the season
Of darkness and stars.
The cold winds whisper
Her name in the twilights;
The empty woods listen
For the first hiss of snow.
Clasp hands together,
Link life to life;
Where the year-flames fade
Listen for the message
In the dry rustling reeds.

Noel-Anne Brennan

The owls sweep forth

In the lengthening nights:

Listen hard.

It is shining

Among dark mists.

February's Country

Initiation into Winter

Here
We enter darkness.
Under the trees like torches
We find the spiral path,
Under the moon
Of the waning year
We find our way.

Deeper we go,
Leaving tokens
At each check-point:

Noel-Anne Brennan

Here lavender thought,

There indigo sight,

And azure speech

And love like emeralds,

And the sounds of winds and seas.

All the summer rainbow of ourselves,

All the rich scents

And memories

Fade and fade.

Hunted by owls

And haunted by dreams

We find our way

By smoky touch alone

Down to the place

Where we lose that, too,

And all is perfection.

In that barren place,

February's Country

In the sterile egg
Where we are left hanging
Under withered trees,
We dream no longer.

But even in perfect silence
Water drips on stone,
Touches our lips.
The wheel shifts slightly
And we grope forward.
We find our way,
Reclaim lost rainbows
Color by color,
And exit darkness
Into winter white.

Noel-Anne Brennan

Solstice

After the solstice
There is no thaw,
But deeper cold.
Yet I feel the light grow longer in my heart,
Ray by ray
Creeping
Across the barren dry
Of winter membrane.
Thin desiccation of soul:
No water springs
From that deep-frozen source.

February's Country

Yet spring there is,

Or will be

(Some far future wet

With torrents from the heartlands.)

The light grows stronger

Ray by painful ray,

Still too weak

For flood-burst heat.

Noel-Anne Brennan

Power Song

The horns of the waxing moon
Curve in my soul;
The willow inspires me
With water and moonlight.
The wind is my pillow
Through the dusk of the violet sky
While the power sings, sings
In the wilderness of
My blood and brain.

February's Country

East

Yellow silk

Through the arch of morning:

Dawn blooms

Like a saffron rose,

Silent

In the house of winds.

Noel-Anne Brennan

Planet Music

In dreams I see the trees
And hear them,
All leafy green-ness
Against the shaded blue of skies,
Whispering earth-songs
To the changing light
With subtleties of color,
The flickered, leafy undersides
Of planet music,
The vibrant, fluid, windy songs.
But also there are harmonies of rock:

February's Country

The song of quartz, the fire frozen,

The blood of earth congealed,

The cold flames clinging,

Remembering heat,

The arrogant crystalline

Heart of the land,

Stony chords

That sing in the bones of life,

The structure and framework

For melodies of air and seas and trees.

Noel-Anne Brennan

Affinities

I begin to feel affinities with summer.
Heat, and the silence
Of working in the garden,
Hot sun bleaching my hair,
Legs swelling
With insect bites.
Lush scent
Of the richness of the earth.
Rabbits watch me placidly:
I have become the meadow,
Natural

February's Country

As tree or stone.

I begin to feel affinities with summer.
I have taken to watching
Wildflowers in the meadow,
Vegetables in the garden.
I catch little dreams
In the corners of my mind,
Edges of elusive joy,
Of fleeting summer promises,
Times out of legend,
Like lakes half-hidden in the woods
Or a bird
Rising out of a field at dawn.

Noel-Anne Brennan

Following the Beacons

I have been sitting inside
All day, while the rain
Streaked windows
Thundered silence
Into my blood.
Now in the aftermath
The light lies over the forest
Like smoke and grey pearls.
Tigerlilies burn
In the soft grey air,
Cold vegetable fire

February's Country

Rising from dark roots,

Heating my lethargy,

Burning fog from the soul.

Flowers and forest

Are beacons into dusk

And birdsongs promise intangibles,

Something half-remembered

Around the hidden corners of thought.

I will follow all beacons,

All the clues,

Let the orange fire rise

Like flowers in my brain,

Upward from dark roots.

Remembrance waits somewhere

In the dusk and the dream,

The grey light after storm.

Noel-Anne Brennan

Western Dream

In twilight
Like the heart
Of an amethyst jewel
The sea sings
Against the shore:
Green songs against the rocks,
Salt songs
Of the vast horizons.
Time dissolves:
What was and will be
In currents and flux.

February's Country

What is real?

The song of the sounding whale,

The leap of dolphins

Against the moon.

Noel-Anne Brennan

Dawn

Visions of springtime

Flow in the winds of dawn,

Little flames

Of yellow air

Caressing the edges

Of winter's kingdom.

Against the sleeping freezing land

The east winds whisper

To the hidden seeds:

Dream deep. Have faith.

February's Country

Trees

In the long twilight of summer

The trees flow

All green and windy

Toward the coming of night

Noel-Anne Brennan

Auroras

There used to be auroras
In the dark night
And even the twilight.
Now
There is darkness
Only,
And I am silent,
Listening for the lights.

February's Country

The Universal Sea

It lies within us all,

Just at that conscious shore,

Waiting.

Submerge now

To deep indigo,

To lapis blue

All shot with golden stars

That sparkle in the mind,

Soothing and connecting

Into one deep flow,

The universal Sea.

Noel-Anne Brennan

This Is

Wild wind

And the light

That changes,

Grey and gold

In the long grass

In the fields:

Sometimes it seems

That this is all

That's left.

This

Is everything.

February's Country

Summer Night

Sweet summer night.
One AM. Deep night.
Velvet blackness,
And rich warmth.
Silence broken by
Only the songs of crickets
And one angry teen,
Walking down the road,
On the phone
Screaming
At his mother.

Noel-Anne Brennan

One thing is certain:

He did not like

His curfew.

February's Country

The Time-traveling Tourist

I want to watch
The mammoths by the river
Under a cold sun.
I want to catch
The golden glimmer
Of a sabertooth in the grass.
I want to feel the wind
Of a planet rich
In possibilities,

Noel-Anne Brennan

Where humans

Are lightly spread

Among the other

Magical beings.

February's Country

Anger

I am burning
Slowly,
A summer sun
Behind clouds
Ready to shine
Red.

Noel-Anne Brennan

Gaia

I feel the great winds shifting,
The vast seas moving.
The earth within her mantle
Twists slowly
In her sleep.
"You bring change?"
She whispers.
"So do I."

February's Country

Endangered

I am a leopard

Limned in light,

I am a tigress

Asleep in the sun,

I am a cougar

By a silent lake,

A snow leopard

On a mountain ledge.

I am a lioness

In the yellow grass,

A clouded leopard

Noel-Anne Brennan

In the jungle rain,

A jaguar

Waiting in a tree,

A lynx

Hidden in winter snow.

I am these

And more.

I charge you with nothing

But beauty

And intensity.

Act as you must.

www.ingramcontent.com/pod-product-compliance
Lightning Source LLC
Chambersburg PA
CBHW061310040426
42444CB00010B/2573